Original title:
Treasured Timberlines

Copyright © 2025 Creative Arts Management OÜ
All rights reserved.

Author: Vivienne Beaumont
ISBN HARDBACK: 978-1-80567-271-5
ISBN PAPERBACK: 978-1-80567-570-9

Abode of the Forgotten Voices

In the woods where squirrels chatter,
Forgotten tales climb up the ladder.
A raccoon wearing glasses, so wise,
Claims he's the king of all that lies.

Old owls hoot in a befuddled way,
They joke about their youth's decay.
The trees laugh softly, swaying slow,
Claiming they saw it all, you know.

The Breath of the Whispering Woods

The trees all gossip, what a crew,
One's in a big hat, quite askew.
They gossip about the birds' bad dates,
And squirrels debating their nutty fates.

The air is thick with giggles and sighs,
A spider spins tales of daring spies.
Each rustling leaf shares a funny lore,
While mushrooms grumble about the floor.

Hidden Paths of the Timeless Glade

Down hidden trails where fables roam,
A gnome insists he's building a dome.
He trips on roots, spills his tea,
Declaring the forest a grand jubilee.

A mischievous fox tries to outwit,
Claiming he can dance, a bit of a hit.
He trips on a twig and falls in a heap,
The trees all chuckle; they just can't keep.

Canopies of Memory

Beneath the branches, laughter swells,
A bear recounts all his fishy tales.
His friends roll in the grass, laughing loud,
He swears he's the best, even in a crowd.

Starlit nights stir up wild delight,
The critters share jokes 'til the morning light.
But as dawn breaks, they all start to yawn,
And wonder where all their snacks have gone.

Whittle Down the Years

Woodpeckers giggle, they tap and they play,
Knocking on trees, they start their ballet.
Squirrels in hats throw acorns in glee,
While branches hold secrets, oh can't you see?

Rabbits in sneakers hop over the logs,
Winking at turtles, they race through the bogs.
Lumberjacks flex while the forest looks on,
But the trees are all chuckling—they're not even gone!

Drawn in the Grain

The patterns of bark tell tales of the rain,
Whirls and swirls—it's a woodsy campaign.
Trees strut their stuff like they're hitting a show,
With knots that wink slyly, oh don't let it go!

A pine cone rolls by, wearing a grin,
Shouting, "I'm a treasure!"—not quite in the bin.
Vines twist and tangle, a green-hued ballet,
Nature's own circus, come join the fray!

Beneath the Sapling Stars

Under the canopy, critters convene,
Reading old maps that no one has seen.
Fireflies flicker, like little comedians,
Lighting the night with their bright little beacons.

The owls gossip softly about the lost loot,
While the raccoons plot mischief in their cute suit.
Stars wink above, they're drawing a line,
As the trees stand tall—oh, isn't it fine?

Nature's Silent Chronicles

Each ring spins a yarn of laughter and cheer,
Tales of tree hugs and whispers we hear.
The forest is busy with giggling delight,
Even the shadows get in on the sight.

The fox wears a cape, prancing with style,
The deer strike a pose, but just for a while.
Branches sway gently, making a cheer,
In the wood's quiet moments, there's fun all year!

The Legacy of Leafy Giants

Tall trees whisper tales of old,
Branches twist like stories told.
Squirrels prance with acorn hats,
While woodpeckers dance like acrobats.

Roots like fingers, grasping tight,
To the secrets hidden out of sight.
One tree yawned, a bird flew in,
"I swear they think I'm full of sin!"

Unraveling the Tapestry of Time

Knots and curls in every trunk,
Like laughter caught in earthy junk.
The breeze should take a gentle bow,
For every branch does take a vow!

Fungi chuckle wearing hats,
Elves recruit their dancing rats.
Moss gets jealous, wants a crown,
While roots debate who's really down!

A Pool of Green Reflections

Leaves peek down from vibrant heights,
Making faces, what a sight!
The sun is laughing, beams a joke,
"Why did the tree get up to poke?"

Rippling waters giggle back,
As frogs leap in their splash attack.
A moose floats by, a grassy boat,
"This is quite the toad-ally funny quote!"

Finding Peace in the Fabled Grove

A gentle breeze with ticklish glee,
Makes every branch dance like a spree.
In this grove, dreams loudly beam,
Even squirrels plot a comic scheme!

Gnomes trade jokes beneath the shade,
While shadows play a fun charade.
Nature's laughter fills the air,
Who knew trees could be so rare?

Guardians of Forgotten Trails

In the woods where squirrels plot,
A raccoon steals a donut, hot!
Old trees grumble, roots entangle,
While branches gossip, laughter wrangle.

Behold a deer upon a spree,
Sneaking snacks like it's a jubilee!
Mice debate on cheese and pie,
While owls hoot their alibi.

Beneath the canopy, nuts collide,
As woodpeckers laugh, filled with pride.
The path is clear with laughter shared,
Each critter plays a role, well-faired.

So tiptoe softly through this space,
Join in the fun, a wild chase!
In forgotten trails, life's a ride,
With giggles echoing far and wide.

Dreams Weaved in Wood.

In a treehouse high, dreams take flight,
A squirrel dreams of a pizza night.
While branches sway in silly dance,
Woodpeckers join, lost in a trance.

Acorns whisper secrets, oh so sly,
As falling leaves bid the sun goodbye.
Bugs break into a merry song,
An ensemble cast of nature's throng.

Rabbits gather with wild tales,
Of mighty hops and misty gales.
Under stars that shine like gold,
Each dream is a treasure, yet untold.

So build your dreams in boughs so wide,
In every twist, let laughter ride.
With wooden dreams that rarely fade,
In the forest's arms, joy's parade.

Whispers of the Ancient Woods

Old trees wear beards of lichen gray,
They chuckle softly at the fray.
A fox recites, with flair and wit,
Ancient lore of playful skit.

Beneath the boughs, the mushrooms chat,
As turtles join, all poised and stat.
A hidden pond bursts into cheer,
With frogs that croak a song sincere.

Breezes carry secrets so slight,
As shadows play, oh what a sight!
Rustling leaves lend a merry shout,
While critters laugh and leap about.

So wander deep where stories grow,
In woods where youth keeps spirits aglow.
The whispers call, a joyful jest,
In ancient realms, we're truly blessed.

Veils of Verdant Canopies

Under layers of leafy dreams,
A raccoon stumbles on chocolate creams.
The sun peeks through in beams so bright,
As chipmunks banter, hearts take flight.

Between trunks, shadows skip and hop,
A hedgehog's got a dance to pop!
With laughter echoing all around,
In leafy veils, joy can be found.

Branches sway like dancers bold,
Tales of whimsy begin to unfold.
In a trunk, a party's held,
A secret world that joy upheld.

So come along to this leafy spree,
Join the laughter, wild and free!
In canopies where fun takes lead,
Nature's jesters grow and seed.

The Pulse of the Verdant Realm

In the realm where greens do shake,
Trees dance and laugh, make no mistake.
They sway to tunes of winds so wild,
Their branches mimic a playful child.

Roots gossip low beneath the ground,
Telling tales of squirrels, dreams unbound.
Leaves tickle each other in delight,
As owls hoot jokes well into the night.

Splendor of the Swaying Oaks

Oh mighty oaks, with crowns so high,
Swinging slowly, watch the clouds go by.
Their acorns drop like jokes from above,
Falling on heads, trees drastically shove.

In the summer, orbs of shade they bring,
While critters beneath begin to sing.
Squirrels in suits, a leafy parade,
Keeping us laughing in their leafy glade.

Lament of the Withering Birch

Once fierce and bright, with a laugh so loud,
Now a whisper beneath the cloud.
Branchless jokes in its fading bark,
But still it chuckles in the dark.

Birds perch high, making puns on pine,
While the birch sighs about old times.
"Oh to be young," it may grumble with flair,
But offers shade for all, still a good pair.

Whispers of the Weathered Trunks

Ancient trunks hold secrets untold,
Sharing giggles, through ages old.
Saplings tease with a cheeky cheer,
While wise old timber lends an ear.

Moss-covered laughter drips from the boughs,
It's the best comedy show, take a bow!
In nature's heart, the jokes never stop,
As the woodlands chuckle, we can't help but hop.

The Spirit of the Fallen Leaves

Once I saw a leaf that danced,
Twisting to catch the wind's advance.
It spun and swirled, what a sight,
Said, 'I'm off to join the kite!'

The ground said, 'Why don't you stay?'
But the leaf just laughed, 'Not today!'
I felt a tickle on my nose,
And sneezed—oh no! Here comes my prose!

A squirrel laughed and chewed a nut,
Said, 'You're alright, just a little cut!'
A leap, a bound, then off he went,
Leaving behind a leaf's lament.

So watch the leaves, their silly games,
Their twirls and flips, all sorts of claims.
For in their fall, a joy we share,
A dance of whimsy in the air!

Luminescent Glades

In the glades where the frogs like to sing,
They croak in chorus, it's quite the thing.
Underneath the glow of a bright moonbeam,
They dream of flies in an airborne theme.

The fireflies join, with their lanterns aglow,
But the frogs croak louder, 'Hey, take it slow!'
They form a band and play all night,
While owls hoot along, what a funny sight!

A rabbit hops in with a laugh so loud,
Said, 'You all look like a glittery crowd!'
They paused for a moment, then ribbited back,
With beats so catchy, you'd think they could rap!

So if you wander where the critters convene,
The luminescent glades are quite the scene.
A dance-off ensues, oh what a delight,
In moonlit giggles until morning light!

Reflections in the Woodland Waters

In the pond where the frogs keep an eye,
They practice ballet, oh my, oh my!
With flippers flailing in gleeful spree,
They claim the stage, just a frog and me!

The fish just smirk and swim with style,
They're the judges, with a wink and a smile.
But every splash brings a frog's loud cheer,
Said, 'Join the party, there's space right here!'

A turtle strolls by, looking for fame,
Said, 'I'm the slowest, but join the game!'
With a splash down the center, they whirl and spin,
What a riot! Each laugh feels like a win.

So if you see a frog do a jig,
With a turtle's slow pace and a fish's big gig,
Remember the joy in the woodland's calls,
Reflections of fun that delights us all!

The Art of Knotted Branches

In the forest where the old trees twist,
They argue over who has the best wrist.
'A spiral here and a twist so fine,'
Said the oak, 'Check out this new design!'

While the birch rolled its eyes and gave a clap,
'Oh please, you're just a gnarled old chap!'
With curls and knots, they laughed in glee,
Said, 'We're all quite slick, don't you agree?'

A raccoon wandered by, all fluff and fun,
Chimed in saying, 'Oh, I've got a pun!'
'If trees wear rings, and branches weave tales,
Then surely we're starting a growth of sales!'

So when you stroll through the wiggly wood,
Remember the knots, as the wise trees stood.
A twist of humor in nature's embrace,
Knotted branches bring a smile to our face!

The Whims of Wooded Spirits

In the woods where shadows dance,
Squirrels wear hats as they prance.
Mice drink tea from tiny cups,
While chipmunks host quirky hiccup ups.

Trees gossip in leafy sighs,
Wandering bees with silly ties.
A raccoon laughs 'til he drops,
As a log rolls by with comical hops.

Owl jokes make the branches sway,
Frogs rhyme in their own funny way.
Every twig knows the woodland tales,
Where laughter rings and humor prevails.

So let's join in, let's be a fool,
Dance around like it's our school.
Embrace the fun that nature gives,
In the woods, the laughter lives.

Shadows Through the Timeless Trees

Beneath the boughs, a shadow slips,
A turtle dons some laughing quips.
With broken branches as his stage,
   He tells a joke that won't age.

The owls hoot with chuckling grace,
As shadows play a funny game of chase.
Rabbits hop in a madcap race,
   With goofy grins on every face.

The sun peeks through, a smile so bright,
   And tickles leaves with sheer delight.
As shadows dance like silly mimes,
   The forest giggles, lost in chimes.

Here among the mighty trees,
All have fun with utmost ease.
In this realm of whimsy spun,
The shadows twirl, and we've just begun.

The Allure of Twisted Timber

Oh, the trunks that twist and twine,
With knobby knees, they love to shine.
A wooden parrot sings off-key,
While a beaver leans back for tea.

Branches bend with a laughing grin,
Giving shade to a piglet's spin.
The knotty roots play peek-a-boo,
As the trees wiggle, 'Look at you!'

A carvings' dance, a funky beat,
Wooden critters shuffle their feet.
With every creak, they share a joke,
As saplings giggle, each one pokes.

Come behold this funny land,
Where timbered spirits take a stand.
With each twist and every turn,
The allure of laughter runs and burns.

Luminescence in the Leafy Shadows

In shadows deep where giggles thrive,
Glowworms shimmer, insects jive.
A firefly dons a disco ball,
While crickets sing a silly call.

Leaves rustle with a whisper light,
As raccoons improvise each night.
A dandelion wears a crown,
While butterflies laugh and spin around.

Underneath the moon's soft glow,
The mushrooms take it nice and slow.
A fairy drops her glitter stash,
And all the critters come to crash.

So come and play in the silver beams,
Where trees whisper all the dreams.
In leafy shadows, joy resides,
As nature's humor gently glides.

Emblems of Enduring Charm

In a forest of dreams, the trees wear a grin,
They gossip with squirrels about where they've been.
Branches are twisted, like stories untold,
Each ring tells a tale that's priceless and bold.

Bouncing along is a raccoon in style,
He dances on roots, oh, canines revile!
The laughter of leaves rustles through the air,
While owls roll their eyes, thinking life isn't fair.

A beaver's grand plans, with logs piled askew,
Calls it art, while the fish just pursue.
In this woodland gala, all creatures partake,
Dancing and prancing for the fun's own sake.

So here's to the trees, in their quirky array,
Reminding us all to be silly and sway.
Among their oddities, laughter does bloom,
In the shade of their charm, we'll dance to our tune.

Echoing Through Ages of Growth

The trees kick the dust, with roots in the air,
They've heard all the jokes, and they never despair.
With a shake of their trunks, they crack silly puns,
While critters below get the punch lines for funs.

From saplings to giants, they lean side to side,
Hosting a party, the forest is wide!
The pine cones are hats, on the heads of the jays,
As they squawk out the news of their clumsy ballet.

They whisper of seasons and wear colorful coats,
Flaunting their bark like they're voting for votes!
A wily old fox joins the line for some dance,
Stumbling yet charming in a picturesque trance.

So celebrate trees in their whimsical way,
With echoes of laughter that brighten the day.
For in every bough and in every wild sound,
A saga of joy in the woodlands is found.

The Symphony of Soft Pines

Soft pines sing tunes like a wash in the breeze,
With needles like flutes, they're a band of experts, please!

Chipmunks on maracas and owls on the mic,
Their rhythm's contagious; who knew a tree liked?

Old oaks claim the solos, all gnarled and grand,
While the willows sway softly, the best dance band.
Branches do the cha-cha, as shadows applaud,
In this woodsy assembly, there's no time to nod!

Mosses are the fans, they cheer from the floor,
With mushrooms as groupies wanting just one encore!
Hedgehogs in tuxedos pop corks with their spines,
As the symphony softens, they toast all the pines.

So come join the party, the nature-made show,
Where laughter and music are free to bestow.
In the heart of the grove, our spirits arise,
As we dance with the woodlands beneath sunny skies.

Breath of the Enchanted Grove

In the grove, wise trees share an old fable,
Of mushrooms that giggle and squirrels at the table.
With acorns as treats and nectar in cups,
They feast on the laughter, as woodland cheers up.

A dapper old turtle struts with such flair,
Claiming he knows the best route in the air.
While butterflies flutter, quite lost in their waltz,
The branches shake gently, like rings made of quartz.

The grass tickles toes, and the sun plays along,
With shadows that dance to an unending song.
Every gust of fresh air tells secrets so sweet,
Turns giggles to whispers, a magical treat.

So breathe in the fun, let your spirit take flight,
In this enchanted space, where wrong feels just right.
From laughter to joy, we savor it all,
For we're part of this tale, and we're having a ball!

A Canvas of Swaying Serenity

In the forest where trees sway,
Leaves dance like they're on holiday.
Branches giggle with a creaky tune,
Rabbits frolic, under the laughing moon.

Squirrels bicker over acorn loot,
While woeful owls wear a solemn suit.
An artful breeze brushes with flair,
Nature's joke is spun through the air.

Sunbeams tickle the barky skin,
Like playful fingers, they gently spin.
Pinecones tumble with comedic flair,
As nature chuckles, without a care.

The Color of Silence in the Woods

When silence paints the forest floor,
It splashes hues like laughter's roar.
A deer trips over a wayward root,
While nearby, a skunk finds a suited suit.

Mossy carpets underfoot squish,
As critters meet for a tasty dish.
They gather round, all quite absurd,
Each discussing the silliest word.

Colors swirl in a breezy fight,
As butterflies giggle, taking flight.
The trees laugh softly, swaying so grand,
In this quiet canvas, life is unplanned.

Resonance of the Rising Canopy

High above, the branches argue,
Debating who should offer view.
A chipmunk quips, 'Hold on, not so fast!'
As they joust in shadows that dart and blast.

Beneath the canopy's swirling green,
A flurry of critters puts on a scene.
Robins serenade with a silly tune,
While a gopher practices its cartoon.

Pine needles rustle, clapping away,
As the squirrels put on a grand ballet.
The dance of nature, both clever and bright,
Turns a quiet moment into pure delight.

Petals and Bark in Harmony

In the garden where petals play,
They gossip about the clouds all day.
A rose blinks pink, while violets laugh,
And daisies yell, 'We're part of the gaff!'

Bark chuckles, holding tales of old,
Of romantic leaves and gossip bold.
Sunflowers salute with comical bows,
While bushes tell tales of curious cows.

The harmony hums in perfect jest,
As nature's crew puts humor to test.
In every bloom and every mark,
There's always a giggle in the park.

A Haven of Lasting Growth

In the forest where laughter blooms,
Trees share secrets in their rooms.
Squirrels giggle in a crazy race,
While branches tickle each other's face.

Mushrooms dance in the soft moonlight,
As owls hoot jokes, with all their might.
A raccoon wears a hat made of leaves,
Pretending he's a king, oh how he believes!

The paths are paved with mossy memes,
Where every twig is bursting at the seams.
Frogs croak puns with all their charm,
Nature's joker, keeping us warm.

Among the pines, the laughter rings,
As they trade tall tales of silly things.
In this woodsy lair, joy never ends,
For the heart of the forest always sends.

The Heartbeat of Nature's Embrace

A woodpecker knocks out a catchy beat,
While rabbits tap dance on dainty feet.
In this space where mirth takes flight,
Every tree is a comedian, what a sight!

Leaves shake hands, all in fun,
Whispers of laughter greet the sun.
Breezes tickle the branches high,
While chipmunks join in, oh my oh my!

The wind is a jester, swaying so free,
Making branches wiggle like they're glee.
A party of nature, wild and bright,
Turning the forest into sheer delight.

Beneath the boughs, friends gather 'round,
Sharing giggles without a sound.
In this realm, joy takes its place,
Nature's laughter, an endless embrace.

Passages Between the Eldest Roots

In the shade of giants, tales unfold,
Saplings lean in to hear the old.
Wisdom flows like a river fine,
With every twist, there's a punchline!

Roots wiggle and dance beneath the ground,
As wise old trees wear crowns profound.
Every knot and gnarled twist,
Holds jokes of seasons that can't be missed.

A snail slides by, its shell a joke,
While bees buzz laughter through each oak.
The blossoms chuckle in the breeze,
Tickled pink by each buzzing tease.

In this realm of deep roots and fun,
Every visit is a home run.
The echoes of laughter between each tale,
Promise that joy's never stale.

Dreams Woven in Wooded Whispers

Beneath the boughs where dreams conspire,
Squirrels plot and conspire to tire.
Twisting tales with every leap,
As shadows giggle, secrets keep.

The fireflies twinkle a dim-lit show,
While branches sway in the evening glow.
A night full of whimsy, no one feels shy,
As trees bend down to share a high-five!

Dreams of nuts and grand escapades,
In a world built from leafy parades.
Where each little critter's got a part,
In this whimsical play that fills the heart.

So let the night roll on with cheer,
With whispers of laughter we hold dear.
In the arms of the woods, we find our way,
A tapestry of joy, woven each day.

Reverie Beneath the Leafy Eaves

A squirrel in a bowler hat,
Doing the cha-cha on a mat.
Acorns dance with a merry grin,
As branches giggle, let the fun begin!

Down below, the ants are spry,
In tiny suits, they strut and fly.
With leaves as umbrellas, they shake and sway,
In their dapper world, they'll never stray!

A twig snaps, a crow lets out a caw,
'Is that a party? Let me see your claw!'
The branches twist to join the beat,
And nature sings with whimsy sweet.

Frogs join in, with leaps sublime,
Croaking rhythms, marking time.
Beneath the eaves, the laughter swells,
In this leafy realm, joy surely dwells!

The Chime of Bark and Breeze

A tree stump lined with jellybeans,
Pipsqueak squirrels in silly scenes.
They play dominoes with fallen leaves,
Cheering loudly, 'Who believes?'

A woodpecker beats a comical tune,
'Tap tap tap, I'll drum till noon!'
But wait! A raccoon steals the show,
Decked in bling, he put on a glow.

The breeze joins in with a whispering laugh,
As birds craft jokes on their leafy staff.
'There's a worm here, think it'll rise?'
Rolling in laughter, beneath the skies.

All the critters nod in delight,
Hosting a gala from morn till night.
Among the boughs, the banter flies,
In this merry world, joy never dies!

Among the Arched Halos of Oak

A wise old owl in oversized specs,
Counts all the acorns, takes stock of checks.
'Ten for you, and three for me!',
With such accounting, it's clear to see!

Chipmunks in capes do daring leaps,
Showing off tricks, while the maple weeps.
'Look at us run, we're fast, we swear!'
While branches sway with such silly flair.

A hedgehog dons a tiny crown,
Declaring himself the king of the town.
With a prickly parade, they traverse the ground,
Reveling in laughter, a joy so profound.

In this realm where whimsy blends,
Under arched halos, the fun never ends.
From oak to oak, let the laughter soar,
In this jubilant jamboree, forevermore!

Curiosities of the Canopied Land

In a world where flowers wear hats,
And dancing mushrooms make witty chats.
The daisies giggle, the roses play,
While the sunbeams twirl at the break of day.

A frog with a bowtie croaks a jest,
Saying, 'I'm the finest, just like the rest!'
With whimsical flair, the critters all glance,
At the peculiar fun of their daily dance.

Fireflies twinkle in rhythm divine,
Creating patterns, a glowing line.
While butterflies flap in a comic duel,
They whirl and twirl, just like in school!

This canopied land, a merry surprise,
A carnival of joy beneath bluest skies.
With each curious turn, the laughter expands,
In this blooming paradise, where glee demands!

Boughs That Bend with Time

In a forest of giggles, where branches sway,
Old whispering trees joke about the day.
They tell tales of squirrels with style so grand,
Who strut through the woods like they own the land.

With acorn hats and a wily grin,
They dance through the leaves, inviting you in.
The trunks crack up as the winds start to tease,
Wobbling knee-deep in the soft, laughing breeze.

Mossy logs chuckle, a comfy old chair,
As critters hold court, with stories to share.
Laughter runs wild, like a creek in a race,
Nature's own stand-up, setting the pace.

Through sunsets wrapped in orange and gold,
Woodland antics remain brave and bold.
So come sit a spell 'neath the bending trees,
And join in the fun, if you laugh with the leaves.

The Canopy's Gentle Hush

Up high in the treetops, a squirrel will shout,
'Watch my acorn juggle!' then spins all about.
While owls in their wisdom nod off for a nap,
And the wind just chuckles, 'What a funny chap!'

A raccoon with style, in a vest made of bark,
Breaks into a dance with a humorous spark.
The branches are clapping as critters chime in,
While the forest's own symphony plays with a grin.

Soft rays of sunshine peek down through the leaves,
Where laughter is rustling and no one believes.
A leaf falls down gently, but it's not quite alone,
The joke of the day leads the acorn on loan.

So come to the woods for a visit, you see,
Where the laughs are contagious, wild, and free.
In this patch of green wonder, shy giggles arise,
A canopy's secret, hiding sweet surprise.

Where the Old Spirits Roam

In a grove where the chuckles roll soft as a breeze,
And the shadows do tango, putting minds at ease.
Old spirits in flannel, with wrinkled green faces,
Whisper punchlines in mystical spaces.

They huddle like fog as they share tale and jest,
Of mushrooms in tuxedos, at nature's own fest.
With fireflies glowing in a carefree dance,
Even the foxes are caught in the trance.

Bark-clad gigglers all sway in delight,
In this peculiar forest, oh what a sight!
Branches with laughter, twirling with glee,
And a soundtrack of nature sets everyone free.

So if wandering through woods feels a bit formless,
Listen close for the chuckles, the spirit of wholeness.
For under the leaves where the laughter can bloom,
Old spirits keep joking, dispelling all gloom.

Footprints on the Woodland Floor

Every step on the earth tells a tale of delight,
From hustle of rabbits to the deer's graceful flight.
Squeaky shoes on the pine needles sound out,
While the trees giggle softly, filled with good sprout.

A bunny hops by, with an ear-to-ear grin,
Playing tag with the shadows, it's a win-win.
These are the paths where the jests do abound,
Echoed in footfalls, a joyful surround.

From squirrels flinging nuts in a playful fray,
To dancing chipmunks just shooing gray away.
The woodland floor whispers of mischief and fun,
In this playful kingdom, you're never outdone.

So wander through woods, where the laughter takes flight,
With every light step, and every slight bite.
In footprints of joy, see the stories that grow,
A tapestry woven in nature's own show.

Echoes in the Silent Grove

In the woods where no one peeks,
A squirrel wears shoes and squeaks.
He dances with style, a comical twist,
While birds go 'Hey! Wait, we're all missed!'

A tree stump tells tales of days gone by,
Of animals trying to learn how to fly.
They trip over roots, in their daring quest,
Yet laughing out loud, they forget the rest.

A chipmunk's on stage with a bright-hued tie,
Offering acorns, 'Try them! Oh my!'
The owls hoot softly, their eyes rolling wide,
'We came for the show but forgot our pride!'

So here in the grove, where giggles arise,
Nature's humor is clear, no need for disguise.
From pinecones that bounce to branches that bow,
It's a comedy club, and we're all in for a show!

Sylvan Memories

Once I saw a rabbit with cake on his nose,
He invited the hedgehogs for afternoon woes.
They sat on green leaves sipping mint tea,
While frogs serenaded with jazz harmony!

A beaver in booties danced over the brook,
Performing a jig by an old, gnarly nook.
The fish burst in laughter, creating a splash,
'Just wait til you see his birthday bash!'

The wise old owl took notes with a pen,
'Please don't tell the squirrels, or they'll join in again!'
Each leaf giggled lightly in the gentle breeze,
Sharing secrets from boughs, amidst the tall trees.

These sylvan memories filled with delight,
Remind us all to enjoy our own flight.
With a chuckle and grin, the forest does play,
Encouraging wonders, both wild and cray!

The Song of the Wind-kissed Trees

The trees sway and sing, oh what a sound,
Like an orchestra formed from the roots underground.
A gust gave a giggle, now branches just sway,
'Watch out for the squirrels that steal all the hay!'

A wobbly willow tried to execute turns,
While maples and oaks pitched in for their burns.
They tripped over twigs, causing quite the scene,
'Stop, you clumsy giants, you're too in between!'

The pine's needles whispered sweet nothings and jests,
Switching partners for dances, just like in the quests.
With laughter echoing in the sun's golden glare,
Together they shimmer in nature's affair.

What songs will they sing when the dawn starts to rise?
Each melody gifted with giggles and sighs.
For the wind-kissed trees weave tales full of mirth,
In a playful embrace of the forest's sweet berth!

Lullabies of the Forest Floor

Beneath the tall ferns where the critters all snore,
Lie tales of a snail who received a world tour!
He rode on the back of a sleepy old fox,
Singing lullabies 'neath the tall ticking clocks.

An ant with a blanket shared dreams of the stars,
While toads croaked along from their mossy old bars.
With crickets composing a symphonic hum,
The forest's soft dreams hid a sneaky old drum.

With mushrooms like pillows in a snug little nook,
The hedgehogs are sleeping, by nature's own book.
Each leaf acts as pages, flipping in the night,
While shadows dance slowly, by moon's silver light.

So close your two eyes, let your dreams soar and twirl,
Join in the laughter of this woodland whirl.
For lullabies echo when the stars start to peep,
In the woods where the giggles still quietly creep!

Flickers of Dawn Among the Boughs

In the morning light, trees stretch wide,
A squirrel on a branch, wearing pride.
With twigs for a crown and leaves for a cape,
He rules the forest, no need to escape.

Birds chirp gossip, setting the scene,
While ants march proudly, acting like queens.
Sunbeams play tag with shadows so spry,
As grasshoppers jump with a laugh in the sky.

The brook giggles softly, tickling feet,
While rabbits hop past with snacks to eat.
Nature's circus, what a delight,
Fluffy clouds cheer on the playful flight.

So come, let's join the fun parade,
Where laughter echoes and worries fade.
Among the branches, life is a song,
In this leafy kingdom, we all belong.

The Stillness of Green Thrones

In dappled shade, the trees sit tall,
With roots like tales that whisper and call.
Their bark is like armor, tough and wise,
Within wooden thrones, their kingdoms rise.

A chubby raccoon wears a mask so sly,
Stealing berries, he giggles a sly lie.
While the owls above, in judgment, stare,
With wisdom and mischief, they're quite a pair.

The wind plays jokes, tickling the leaves,
As nature weaves patterns that nobody believes.
The mushrooms dance, in their polka-dot best,
Inviting all critters for a fun-filled fest.

Here in the stillness, laughter finds grace,
In the shade of these thrones, we all find our place.
Let's toast with acorns and joyfully sing,
For in this green kingdom, we're all living kings.

Nature's Handcrafted Stories

Each branch a pencil, each leaf a page,
Writing tales of fun — not war or rage.
A caterpillar spins stories with flair,
While a curious snail takes its time to compare.

Bees buzz in circles, telling their dreams,
While frogs croak ballads beside silver streams.
The flowers giggle, colors bright and bold,
As butterflies flutter, their tales unfold.

The sun sets low, with a cheeky wink,
As crickets compose a tune to rethink.
Each twig holds a secret, a laugh or a sigh,
In nature's gallery, time flies by.

So gather around, let the stories unfold,
In this forest of laughter, where life is gold.
With each tale crafted, let's laugh until night,
For nature's own stories are pure delight.

Veins of Sapphire in the Forest

In the heart of the woods, a river does gleam,
Like ribbons of sapphire, a shimmering dream.
Raindrops giggle, splashing with glee,
As bushes sway lightly, dancing with the spree.

Owls in their hoots share a comical jest,
While turtles in mud take a long, lazy rest.
The fish flash their scales, putting on quite a show,
As dragonflies zoom in a frenetic flow.

Moss carpets the ground, a soft, bouncy seat,
Inviting us all for a picnic retreat.
So bring out your sandwiches, make it a feast,
For among these fine woods, joy has increased!

With laughter echoing, the forest sings on,
As creatures unite in this merry dawn.
In veins of sapphire, we frolic and play,
In this wild wonder, let's cherish the day.

Echoes Between the Pines

In the forest where the squirrels dance,
Laughter ripples with every glance.
A woodpecker taps a silly beat,
While rabbits hop on tiny feet.

The trees gossip with rustling leaves,
Sharing secrets the old pine weaves.
Beneath their shade, the critters play,
In their own quirky, wild ballet.

Each branch bows low with playful glee,
As chipmunks make their bold decree:
"We'll build a castle in the sky!"
A fortress where the acorns fly.

So if you wander through this green,
And spot a scene that's quite a scene,
Just know the woods are laughing still,
With every wind that gives a chill.

Roots of Resilience

Down below where stories twine,
Roots dig deep and intertwine.
Each wriggle holds a funny tale,
Of how they won the crazy gale.

One found a shoe, a sole so grand,
Another yanked a lost watering can.
While worms wiggle in a chomping race,
Caterpillars chuckle at their slow pace.

As trees stand tall with sturdy pride,
They hoist their limbs up to the side.
"Look, I'm taller!" one cries out,
While branches sway and wiggle about.

And when the winds let out a sigh,
The trees just grin and stand up high.
With roots of resilience all around,
They laugh at storms that try to drown.

Shadows of Silent Sentinels

In the stillness of the evening light,
Shadows stretch with a playful fright.
Each tree a guard, a silent prank,
With branches dipped in laughter's flank.

They lean and bend with a creaky wit,
Whispering jokes in the twilight bit.
"Why did the acorn cross the glade?"
To teach the oaks the waltz they made!

A fox trots by with a cheeky grin,
As shadows peek out from thickened skin.
"What's black and white and a tree's best friend?"
A panda, you see, that loves to blend!

So take a stroll beneath the boughs,
And hear their jokes, you'll laugh, I vow.
For silent sentinels, wise and grand,
Hold chuckles deep like soft, warm sand.

Guardians of the Gnarled Groove

Twisted trunks with stories vast,
Stand in rhythm, each tree a cast.
Guardians of mischief and time's embrace,
They sway and twist with a happy face.

A crow drops by with a loud caw,
While the sycamore scratches its knotted paw.
"Why do we dance?" the elder asks,
"To keep our roots from aching tasks!"

In grooves so deep, the laughter flows,
As nature's humor constantly grows.
With gnarled arms, they share a wink,
And whisper secrets as you blink.

So if you hear a chuckling breeze,
Know it's the trees, aiming to please.
In their funky groove, they own the night,
Guardians of laughter, pure delight.

Chamber of Familiar Fragrance

In the woods, aromas blend,
A skunk's perfume, oh, what a trend!
Scented air in every nook,
Who needs a map? Just sniff a book!

Bamboo's tickle makes me sneeze,
While rabbits hop, they do as they please.
Each whiff a tale, a laugh, a sigh,
Nature's cologne makes us all fly!

Beeches gossip in softest breeze,
Barking trees are such a tease.
In this chamber of fragrant fun,
I'll trade my nose for a slice of sun!

Twists and turns, sensory delight,
Who knew a forest could be so bright?
So let's frolic, take a chance,
Among the scents, we'll dance and prance!

Veil of the Forest's Keeper

The keeper's cloak, a leafy dress,
Hides squirrels who love to jest.
With acorns flying, oh what a show,
Dancing shadows steal the glow.

Behind the veil, a woodpecker knocks,
Telling secrets to the rocks.
Mice laugh loud at blunders made,
In this wood, there's no charade!

Twisted trunks with grinning faces,
Chatting, laughing in their places.
Who knew trees could crack a joke?
Nature's humor, just bespoke!

The veil of leaves might whisper low,
But in this grove, we steal the show.
With giggles here, beneath the pines,
We're all just kids, sipping sunshine!

Insight from the Elder Trees

Elders stand with wise old grins,
Telling tales of life and sins.
"Don't rush," they say, "take life slow,
Unless you trip on roots—oh no!"

With bark like wrinkles, they recite,
Stop and smell the sap, that's right!
A wise old oak with a knowing stare,
Says, "Drink some rain, don't have a care!"

Thickets thrum with laughter loud,
While hidden frogs jump, so proud.
"Leap a little, enjoy the day,
Join in the fun, come what may!"

So wise trees chuckle in the breeze,
Swaying gently, at perfect ease.
Insights come, both wild and classy,
In these woods, we live so sassy!

Twilight Among the Knotted Roots

Twilight whispers through the trees,
Knotted roots with silly knees.
Dance around, they twist and shout,
Wondering what we're all about.

Fireflies giggle, lighting the way,
Inviting us to join their play.
Beneath the stars, we prance like fools,
A chorus of giggles, breaking rules!

The roots joke about the way they bend,
"Not quite yoga—but we transcend!"
So roots unite, and shadows bloom,
In this twilight, we laugh and zoom!

Join the fun, let laughter sprout,
In nature's field, there's no doubt.
Twilight's magic, a comic sight,
Knotted roots make every night!

Secrets of the Timbered Tapestry

In a forest so grand, owls wear hats,
While squirrels discuss their favorite spats.
Mice dance in shoes made of acorn shells,
Singing sweet tunes of their woodland smells.

A rabbit who juggles with twigs and grass,
Hops on a stump, showing all of his sass.
Tree branches gossip, they creak and sway,
Whispering secrets in a cheeky play.

Raccoons in tuxedos hold midnight feasts,
With berries and nuts, they are quite the beasts.
They toast with thimbles, their laughter so loud,
While nearby, the beetles form a proud crowd.

At dusk, when the sun dips, they start their show,
In funny old costumes they dance to and fro.
With giggles and jiggles, the forest alive,
In a world of their own, oh how they thrive!

The Dance of Shifting Shadows

The shadows wiggle with glee by the trees,
Doing a two-step, as light breezes tease.
A raccoon in a cape leads the brigade,
Stumbling and fumbling, he's quite the charade.

Swaying and swinging, they bashfully peek,
Nibbling on donuts made of ripe leek.
The moon's their DJ, spinning tracks on repeat,
While fireflies join in with rhythmic beat.

The fox in a top hat shows off his flair,
With a twirl and a spin, he dances on air!
Laughter echoes as shadows unite,
Casting wild forms in the cool moonlight.

In this madcap dance, all creatures abound,
Even shy hedgehogs come out with a bound.
They trip and they tumble, they share a good laugh,
The night full of fun, and shadows in half!

The Lullaby of Leaves

Leaves wiggle and giggle on branches up high,
Whispering secrets as breezes pass by.
They hum a sweet tune, their voices so light,
Making the woodland feel cozy and bright.

A leaf slipped and fell, doing flip after flip,
Joined by a buddy, they twirled on a trip.
They landed on mushrooms, a soft, lovely bed,
Sharing the tales that the wise tree had said.

Frogs croaked a chorus, the squirrels chimed in,
A melody born from the heart of their kin.
With twigs in their paws, they formed a great band,
Playing on stumps beneath the tree's stand.

As nightfall approaches, they slow down the song,
Nestling together, where they all belong.
The lullaby softens, the stars start to gleam,
In a world made of whispers, they drift into dreams.

In the Heart of the Green Abyss

In the green abyss, where the oddballs roam,
Lizards wear glasses discussing their home.
Frogs in tuxedos leap from log to log,
Sharing wise tales over coffee with a hog.

A hedgehog with glasses reads books by the creek,
While owls critique him, they're rather oblique.
"Your plot is too thin!" one hooted with cheer,
And the hedgehog just chuckled, "I'll stick to the beer."

Fireflies flit by, acting like they own
The dance floor of dusk, with a starry throne.
Dancing to tunes that only they know,
Sporting glow-in-the-dark on their tails, what a show!

But when the moon rises, they all hit the hay,
Dreaming of shenanigans for another day.
In the heart of green, with laughter in store,
They giggle and wiggle, then rest—who could ask for more?

Whispers of Worn Branches

Among the trees, the squirrels jest,
Pinecones fall, they think it's a test.
A raccoon laughs at the woodpecker's knock,
Says, "Buddy, chill! It's just a block!"

Bark bits tumble like jokes unpinned,
Branches sway, their laughter thinned.
Trees start chortling, roots in a dance,
As leaves giggle, they flurry and prance.

The owl winks, and the sun peeks by,
"Why do trees never ask why?"
They stretch out limbs, bask in the sun,
Adding punchlines to a punny run.

In this wild wood, they throw a bash,
Where whispers twirl and gaggles clash.
With every breeze, a chuckle must raise,
Nature's comedy, in leafy displays.

Echoes Amongst the Leaves

Leaves chatter softly, a rustling game,
"What's the best way to get a tree's fame?"
"Just drop your acorns, make a loud thump,
And tell all the critters to gather and jump!"

Branches sway, they sway with glee,
Tickling each other, just wait and see.
A dandelion rolls up, joins the fun,
"Plant your feet, here's how we run!"

The sunbeam laughs, it wiggles a ray,
Bidding the shadows to join in the play.
A gust of wind shouts, "Catch me if you can!"
The trees all giggle, "We're part of the plan!"

Whispers blend through the vibrant air,
With every rustle, there's banter to share.
Laughter erupts, it dances on high,
In a glade full of echoes, the folly won't die.

Heartwood's Embrace

Deep in the woods, a stump tells a tale,
Of squirrels who skated, and bunnies who sail.
"My heartwood's heavy, but my smile is light,
Join me for laughs till the fall turns to night!"

With each passing breeze, a funny quirk lifts,
"I swear I just saw a woodpecker with gifts!"
The chipmunks all snicker, the hedgehog rolls near,
"Did you see that old tree trip over a deer?"

Branches bend low, they lean in for fun,
"Let's crown a new king!" "But who's number one?"
The leaves start to giggle; they drift in delight,
"Let's name him 'Barky'! He reigns day and night."

In this cozy circle, laughter remains,
Nature's own punchlines, echo through veins.
With roots intertwined, and stories to share,
The heartwood's embrace wraps within gentle air.

Canopy of Secrets

Under the leaves, the rumors are wild,
A rabbit whispers, "My friend's just a child!"
With branches overhead, gossip takes flight,
"Did you hear about the tree that danced all night?"

The ferns are all blushing, so green, and so bright,
As the sun tickles trunks in broad daylight.
"Secrets up high, they tickle the limbs,
What's life without laughter, or rattling hymns?"

A woodpecker's drumming, off in the back,
Adds rhythm to chatter, as laughter won't lack.
"Why do trees never play poker?" they tease,
"Because they're afraid of losing their leaves!"

With each little rustle and playful exchange,
The canopy giggles, ready to change.
In a world so vibrant, full of delight,
Nature composes, a hilarious sight.

Storylines in the Sunlit Glades

In glades where squirrels dance and prance,
A tree once tried to learn to romance.
But every time it bent to woo,
A branch would bob, and off it flew!

The owls are judges, wise and old,
They laugh at antics, brash and bold.
Aww, look at that! It's quite a scene,
A bachelor tree with hopes so keen!

Nearby, rabbits gossip in a hush,
About a pine that taught a mushroom to blush.
"Was it the sunlight? Or just a joke?"
As woodpeckers chuckle, pecking at oak.

At dusk, they gather, tales to spin,
Of who fell over, and how they did win.
Life's a giggle in these sunlit bows,
Nature's humor, who'd dare to oppose?

The Gravity of Green Majesty

In a forest where trees wear crowns so grand,
One claimed it could dance, but only could stand.
It stomped and it swayed, but roots held it tight,
The flora all chuckled, oh what a sight!

A compass vine tried to find its way,
But got caught in a knot, oh what a display!
The ferns rolled their fronds, laughing in glee,
As the vine begged for help from a wise old tree.

Moss gathered round, spreading tall tales,
Of tripping young saplings on slippery trails.
With gravity's pull and roots in a tangle,
The woods are a circus, a humorous angle!

So raise a glass of nectar to cheer,
For nature's mishaps, we hold dear.
In this green majesty, laughter does reign,
A comedy show with no pause for pain!

Windswept Moments Under Canopies

Beneath the boughs where the breezes twirl,
A twig once tried to become a swirl.
It flipped and it flopped—in a tangled fight,
Only to land on a sleeping kite!

A chattering chipmunk, too proud to hide,
Wore acorn hats, a whimsical guide.
"Nature's runway!" it proclaimed in glee,
But tripped on its tail, with laughter to see.

Leaves rustled softly, sharing a giggle,
As a beetle danced, its moves quite the wiggle.
In the whispers of wind, joy takes its flight,
Moments of whimsy stitch day into night.

For under canopies, life plays its tune,
With memories woven, like a great cartoon.
In windswept laughter, we find our reprieve,
Nature's bright stage where we all believe!

Tales of the Twilight Timber

As night creeps in, the wood speaks low,
Of a lumberjack with quite the show.
With a chainsaw raised and a faux-ballad sung,
The trees all laughed—they loved his fun!

The squirrels formed bands, percussion with nuts,
While the owls hooted, forming big ruts.
A deer joined in, strumming the air,
With twigs for guitars, without a care.

Moonlight's the spotlight for woodland cheers,
As shadows dance and banish all fears.
In twilight's embrace, all worries are slim,
As laughter rings out, a jubilant hymn.

So gather your stories, share them with flair,
For under the stars, we all have our share.
In tales of timber, we paint the night bright,
With giggles and dreams taking glorious flight!

Veins of the Ancient Forest

In the woods where squirrels plot,
Trees gossip secrets, like it or not.
Birch trees dance in the breezy flow,
Maples tell jokes only they know.

With roots entangled, they laugh and sway,
Whispering tales of their youthful play.
Saplings giggle, hoping to grow,
While old oaks grumble, 'Don't take it slow!'

Fungi are the comedians down below,
Tickling the bark with their stealthy show.
Mossy carpets cheer in bright green hue,
"Moss like us? It's a dream come true!"

This forest is wild, a humorous bard,
With punchlines hidden behind every yard.
Crickets chirp tunes of comedic flair,
While stumps hold auditions for the next big heir.

Shadows Beneath the Bark

Silent shadows wiggle and twist,
Beneath the bark, they laugh, they insist.
A raccoon in plaid snickers with glee,
"I'm the king of this log, just wait and see!"

The shadows shimmy when night takes the stage,
Otters bursting forth like a wild rampage.
"Let's throw a party!" the fireflies beam,
As trees roll their eyes, 'Oh, what a dream!'

Squirrels in shades whisper secrets in flight,
"Did you hear the one about the tree in plight?"
Branches sway gently, mocking the claims,
"Seriously? We're just branches, not names!"

The quiet of dusk shines with laughter's embrace,
Echoes of chuckles weave through this place.
Though some say they're merely a trick of the light,
These shadows remind that joy takes its flight.

The Language of the Pines

The pines speak softly in whispers and sighs,
"Do you hear that? It's the beetle's reprise!"
They gather in circles, a conifer crew,
Trading tall tales that are funny but true.

"Cedar can't skate, he falls on his side,
While Spruce puts on curls, he's full of pride!"
Their laughter echoes, a rustling song,
As wind carries jokes where they all belong.

Ferns join the party, with their frilly flair,
Tickling the roots with a twist of their hair.
Old stumps crack jokes about bark and delight,
"Stand up and laugh, it's a woodsy good night!"

Laughter like sunlight bursts from the scene,
In the land of the evergreens, life's evergreen.
For in every whisper, there's joy and a grin,
As the pines remind us to let the fun in!

Roots of Remembrance

Roots reminisce of adventures so grand,
With tales of the past that often get spanned.
"Remember the time we tripped the gardener?"
"Yeah, he fell down, what a real pardoner!"

Now they're all tangled under the ground,
Compiling their mischief, some things they found.
"Who knew a worm could tell such a yarn?
His tales would make Shakespeare's plots feel so worn!"

Grassy knolls chuckle, they can hardly breathe,
"Was it this root that stole last fall's wreath?"
As leaves tumble down in the autumn wind,
Reminiscing of fun is how they begin.

Life teaches laughter, the roots stay bereft,
But joy is the treasure that's always left.
In the soil's embrace, they sing and unite,
Finding humor is pure, as we savor the light.

Songbirds on the Bloodwood Branches

Chirping loud with all their might,
The little songbirds take to flight.
They dance and hop like they're on stage,
In nature's play, they steal the wage.

One plump fellow, quite the clown,
Tripped on a twig and fell right down.
His friends all giggled, oh what a sight,
As he fluffed his feathers, claiming flight!

A parrot with jokes, a real wise guy,
Tells tales of cats who aim too high.
The branches shake with laughter so bright,
In the bloodwood's shade, all feels just right.

When twilight comes, their tunes do fade,
But in our hearts, their pranks are laid.
We close our eyes and dream of cheer,
Until next dawn, when they reappear.

Canopy Dreams in Quiet Glades

Beneath the leaves where sunlight gleams,
Squirrels scamper, chasing dreams.
They stashed their snacks in a leafy nook,
Yet one chewed too much, now he's stuck!

A raccoon laughs with a pastry in hand,
Munching on treats, oh isn't life grand?
He waves at a deer, who gives him a stare,
"Is that a donut? I don't really care!"

The shadows play tricks, creating a spree,
Where flowers gossip like folks at tea.
The petals blush as they overhear,
A bee's wild tale that ends in a sneeze!

Even the breeze finds time for a jest,
Tickling trees in their leafy vest.
With laughter around, the glades come alive,
In this playful world, we all thrive.

Reflections of the Mossy Whisper

In a pond where the lilies recline,
Frogs join in chorus, all out of line.
Ribbit, ribbit, they croak at a fly,
"A bite or a snack? Oh me, oh my!"

A turtle slow, with wisdom to share,
Said, "Hurry up, why go anywhere?"
He waits for the sun, for a warm embrace,
While fish zoom past, a frantic race.

The log that lies beneath the trees,
Whispers to crickets, "Bring me some cheese!"
They laugh and chirp 'til the night's grown old,
In reflections of shadows, stories unfold.

As dusk turns bright with stars on the rise,
Even the fireflies have laughing eyes.
In this mossy nook, near the soft rippling,
It's fun to just sit back and start giggling.

The Forest's Embrace Unfolds

In a forest where the tall trees prance,
Animals gather for a wild dance.
A bear in a tutu leads the way,
While rabbits shout, "Hip-hip-hooray!"

A fox runs circles, oh look at him twirl,
A fox in a hat makes the loggers swirl.
From high up above, an owl just hoots,
"My dear woodland friends, don't forget your boots!"

Down below, a badger sings out of tune,
"Is it evening or morning? I can't find the moon!"
Yet all join in, what a silly parade,
With laughter and jigs, no need for a grade.

As twilight brings in the stars that gleam,
The forest embraces each silly dream.
In this patchwork of joy, let the revelry live,
In every nook, oh, what fun we give!

Timeless Tales of the Wilderness

In a forest where squirrels play,
They argue who's the best at ballet.
The trees giggle, their branches sway,
While the porcupines cheer, 'Hip-hip-hooray!'

A moose wears glasses, looking quite wise,
He reads bedtime stories to raccoon spies.
Their laughter echoes through starlit skies,
As the owls roll their eyes and sighs arise.

A beaver with dreams of being a chef,
Cooks pine cone soup, but it tastes like a mess.
He serves it proudly, with a leafy crest,
The critters just grin, "We're all quite blessed!"

A turtle dances, slow and surreal,
While frogs cheer him on with an enthusiastic squeal.
They host a party to seal the deal,
In the wilderness, joy is the real meal.

Emblems of Resilience

A tiny acorn dreamed to grow tall,
Amongst ancient pines, standing proud and all.
"Watch me," it chirps, though feeling quite small,
"How hard could it be? I'll just recall!"

The stumps tell tales of brave sapling fights,
Against storms and critters in wild, funny tights.
Each day is a new chance for quirky delights,
As the trees bop to unseen rhythms and heights.

A wise old tree, with knots galore,
Tells tales of loggers that came long before.
"I dodged their axes, I've still got the score,
For my roots are deep and my laughter's my core!"

Deer prance about, with new antlers to flaunt,
While birds play tag and don't even taunt.
In this vibrant realm, where silliness haunts,
Nature's strong spirit, in mischief, will daunt.

Beneath the Boughs of Time

Under the branches, a rabbit's got style,
He wears a top hat and walks a fine mile.
He tips it to passing foxes with guile,
While the bear gives a nod, cracking a smile.

The owls hold court, hosting a quiz show,
Where the answers are silly and none really know.
They hoot out the questions, putting on a show,
While all the woodland critters gather below.

A chipmunk DJ spins acorn beats,
Hosting a dance-off with happy little feats.
With toe-tapping rhythms that no one defeats,
In the glow of the moon, everyone competes.

A wise old oak mentions days of yore,
How squirrels once surfed on trees by the shore.
With laughter that echoes, the legends encore,
Beneath the boughs, joy's what we adore.

Sagas of the Solitary Spruce

In a glen lives a spruce, so grand and alone,
He tells epic tales with a beautiful tone.
"Listen close, friends, I'm a tree of renown,
A wooden bard with a leafy crown!"

The forest critters gather near for fun,
To hear of the battles that he's overcome.
"The birds stole my pine cones, they thought it was done,
But I rallied my roots, and look how I've won!"

A raccoon wears shades, calling it cool,
An old log becomes a nature-themed school.
With wisdom that flows, and laughter as fuel,
They learn life's great lessons beneath nature's rule.

So raise a toast to the solitary pine,
For every tall tale and every punchline,
In humor and heart, he's truly divine,
In the saga of laughter, he always will shine.

Cerulean Canopies

In a forest of blue, where the skies collide,
Squirrels plot mischief, with nuts as their pride.
They wear acorn hats, ride branches so high,
Chasing their shadows, as twigs wave goodbye.

The sun laughs aloud, with rays all aglow,
Tickling the leaves as they dance to and fro.
A rabbit prances, with shoes far too tight,
Jumps into laughter, then flips with delight.

A raccoon in shades, sipping dew from a cup,
Tells tales of a bear who just can't get up.
The trees roll their eyes, hold back their own snicker,
As wind joins the giggles, a wise little flicker.

So gather round friends, in this canopy bright,
Where humor and nature create pure delight.
Let's toast to the branches, the splits in the bark,
For laughter is found in each leaf's happy spark.

Age-old Guardians

Beneath the wise eyes of trees standing tall,
They whisper of secrets from seasons of fall.
A pine tips its hat to a sprightly young spruce,
While birches gossip about squirrelly truce.

The mighty old oak, with a voice deep and gruff,
Says, "Younglings, be careful, life's dreadfully tough!"
Yet giggles emerge from the roots of the land,
As laughter erupts from a tiny branch band.

They hold up their limbs like they're trolling for fame,
Each story they share, a ridiculous game.
A walnut slips over, dressed up like a king,
Who trips on his robe, what a comedic thing!

Amidst the wise guardians, with hearts full of cheer,
They chuckle at life, no need for a sneer.
For each scar and knot tells a tale with a grin,
In this quirky old grove, each laugh is a win.

Through the Eyes of an Oak

Oh, the secrets I see from my sturdy old throne,
Where birds spin tall tales and make mock of the moan.
A chipmunk, quite dapper, in his waistcoat and tie,
Proclaims he's a lawyer, oh my, what a guy!

Eagles swoop down with a wink and a plan,
As bluebirds discuss how to start a fan clan.
The insects debate over maps of the ground,
While I'm just here chuckling at all that I've found.

The lightning strikes once, but I never did flinch,
For there's humor in storms if you stop just an inch.
The rain dances merrily, tapping my bark,
While I share a laugh with the faintest of lark.

With each passing season, my branches grow wide,
A witness to giggles that nature can't hide.
So come share your stories, bring joy on the breeze,
Through the eyes of an oak, life's full of such tease.

The Dance of the Evergreens

In a twirl of the pines, where the laughter takes flight,
Dancing trees sway, oh what a glorious sight!
With needles that tickle, they sway to a tune,
While dancers debate how to jive with the moon.

Firs lead the ballroom, with a regal finesse,
The spruce try to keep up, though they tend to excess.
A solo pine wobbles, then slips on a cone,
With all of the elms breaking out in a groan.

The whispers of wind serenade them to sway,
As branches entwine in a whimsical play.
A fox joins the floor, in a flurry of fur,
Spinning with laughter, it's all quite a blur.

So come out and join in this jubilant scene,
Where evergreens gather, and fun's evergreen.
With roots intertwined, they celebrate glee,
In the dance of the evergreens, come dance with me!

www.ingramcontent.com/pod-product-compliance
Lightning Source LLC
Chambersburg PA
CBHW051634160426
43209CB00004B/644